JANE
LONG
TEXAS JOURNEY

bright sky press
HOUSTON, TEXAS

2365 Rice Boulevard, Suite 202,
Houston, Texas 77005

10 9 8 7 6 5 4 3 2 1
Library of Congress Cataloging-in Publication Data

Wade, Mary Dodson.
Jane Long : Texas journey / by Mary Dodson Wade ; Illustrated by Virginia Marsh Roeder.
p. cm. -- (Texas heroes for young readers ; 5)
Includes bibliographical references and index.
ISBN 978-1-933979-39-7 (hardcover : alk. paper)
1. Long, Jane Herbert Wilkinson, 1798-1880--Juvenile literature.
2. Pioneers--Texas--Biography--Juvenile literature. 3. Women pioneers--Texas--Biography--
Juvenile literature. 4. Frontier and pioneer life--Texas--Juvenile literature. 5. Texas--Biography--
Juvenile literature. I. Roeder, Vir   ginia Marsh, ill. II. Title. III. Series.

F389.L85W3295 2009
976.4'05092--dc22
[B]   2009007997

Book and cover design by Cregan Design
Illustrations by Virginia Marsh Roeder
Printed in China through Asia Pacific Offset

JANE
LONG
TEXAS JOURNEY

MARY DODSON WADE

ILLUSTRATIONS BY

VIRGINIA MARSH ROEDER

bright sky press
HOUSTON, TEXAS

TABLE OF CONTENTS

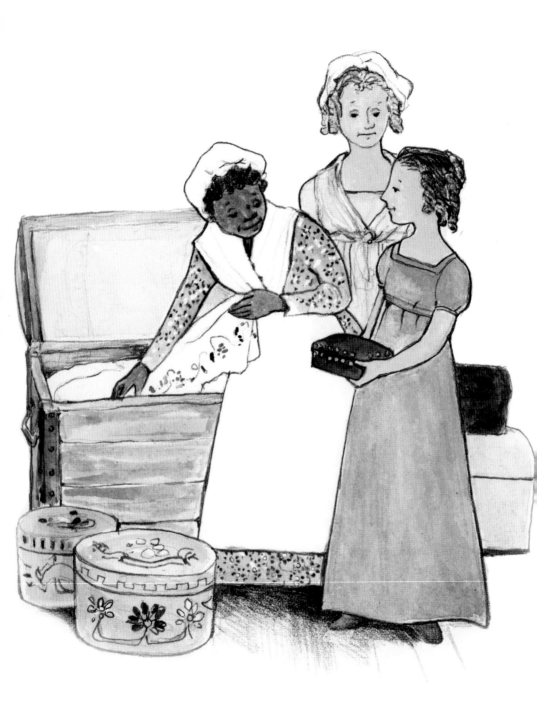

CHAPTER 1

Mississippi and Marriage

Priors Cleve, the Wilkinson home on the Patuxent River in Charles County, Maryland, bustled with activity. Thirteen-year-old Jane Herbert Wilkinson watched as her trunk filled with beautiful dresses. She was leaving the only home she had known.

Jane had been born at Priors Cleve July 23, 1798, in the house her great-great-grandfather had built nearly 100 years before. The beautiful house had wooden paneling from floor to ceiling around the parlor fireplace.

Jane's father, Captain William Mackall Wilkinson,

had run the large tobacco plantation with thirty slaves. But he had died when Jane was about a year old. Now, in 1811, Priors Cleve had been sold. Two of Jane's older sisters had married and moved far away to Mississippi. Jane and her mother, Anne Herbert Wilkinson, were going to live near them.

As the youngest of the ten children, Jane had always been the center of attention. Her mother wanted to make sure she was a proper young lady.

Jane knew how to embroider. She could serve tea gracefully to guests. She became a good dancer and had lots of pretty dresses to wear. But the family spoiled her. Jane always knew what she wanted and made sure that she got it.

With the trunks crammed full and tied securely to the coach, the two climbed in for the long journey. Their destination was Natchez, Mississippi, where Jane's sister Barbara Calvit and her husband Alexander lived.

After a trip that stretched over many weeks, they finally arrived and settled into a place near Barbara's home. With family nearby, Jane's life did not change much. But, a little over a year after they moved, Jane's mother died.

Jane went to live with the Calvits on their plantation. The pretty girl grew into a tall, lively young person with a strong will.

In the spring of 1815 sixteen-year-old Jane was getting ready to leave for school. She had just pulled a green silk bonnet over her dark curls. As she picked up her books to leave for school, one of the servants ran up. She insisted that Jane come see a soldier.

Jane didn't understand why she should bother, but the servant insisted. "This is the handsomest man in the world, and I want you to see him before you go to school."

Just then Dr. James Long came through the door. The tall soldier was a striking figure in his military uniform. The recent American victory over the British at the Battle of New Orleans had ended the War of 1812. Many of the wounded soldiers had been taken to homes along the Mississippi River to recover. One had come to the Calvit plantation, and Dr. Long was there to treat him.

The army surgeon was five years older than the pretty student. He was immediately struck with her beauty. Jane saw at once that the servant was right about the doctor. Putting aside her school books, she took off her bonnet. The two sat by the window and passed the afternoon playing backgammon. The prize was a pair of gloves, and Jane won.

The next day the doctor came again to the plantation. He found Jane and held out the gloves. She refused them, saying it was just a game. Dr. Long insisted, "If you will not take them as your due; you must at least accept them as a present."

As she put them on, he took her hand. He told her that he wished to have the hand that went with the glove. This marriage proposal surprised and flattered her.

The idea of marriage shocked Jane's family. She was so young, and they barely knew the man. But Jane was smitten with the handsome doctor and had made up her mind that she would marry him.

Her family used the argument that she was still a minor. Legally, she needed a guardian. Since both her parents were dead, someone had to make decisions about her well-being. The law, however, allowed a young person to pick anyone they wanted.

When the family confronted Jane about a guardian, she had a ready answer. "You force me to choose, and he is my choice." With James Long as Jane's guardian, the family had no way to stop the headstrong girl.

CHAPTER 2

Following Her Husband

The marriage took place on May 14, 1815, just weeks after the couple met. Jane was not yet seventeen. The Longs moved to a small Mississippi town, and Dr. Long practiced medicine for a while. Jane, however, persuaded him to buy land near Vicksburg, about sixty miles north of Natchez. He gave up medicine and concentrated on running Walnut Hill plantation. Baby Ann Herbert Long was born there in 1816.

A year or so later, the Longs sold Walnut Hill and moved into Natchez. James Long went into business with a partner. The store they operated sold many things including supplies for people moving westward.

Many Americans were unhappy that Spain controlled Texas. They believed that President Jefferson had bought Texas when he made the Louisiana Purchase just a few years earlier. To end the argument over boundary lines, representatives of both countries had signed a treaty. The treaty made Florida part of the United States, but Spain kept Texas. Many Americans, especially those living near the border, did not like the treaty.

A group of men who lived in Natchez were eager to claim Texas as American territory. They were willing to march to Texas and fight if necessary to make it part of the United States. James Long became their leader, and the men prepared to leave.

Jane was not able to go with her husband. It was near time for their second child to be born. Instead, she and her sister Anne Chesley, who lived nearby, made a flag for the soldiers to carry. It had red and white stripes with a red fringe all around. In the upper left corner a large single white star gleamed on a red background.

As crowds cheered and cannon boomed, the little army of seventy-five men marched away. James Long rode at the head of the soldiers.

Only a few days after the men left, baby Rebecca was born. The Longs had been married four years. Jane had never before been separated from her husband, and she was determined to join him. Taking three-year-old Ann and two-week-old Rebecca, she began a trouble-filled trip to Alexandria, Louisana, where her sister Barbara Calvit now lived.

After resting for a month to recover, Jane left the two children in Barbara's care and started toward Texas to join her husband. Near the border at Natchitoches (NACK-uh-tish), Louisiana, American soldiers stopped her and took her trunk. They did not want her to cross the border alone.

They sent word to her husband in Nacogdoches (nack-uh-DOH-chez), Texas, that his wife was at the border. Randal Jones, an experienced wilderness guide, came to escort Jane.

At night they stopped at isolated homes of American squatters. They traveled through drenching rain, swimming their horses across swollen rivers. Jane would not stop until she reached her husband.

In Nacogdoches, Long's army had grown to 300 men. Eager volunteers had joined as the little army made its way across Louisiana. Once the group entered east Texas, they found few settlers and no real towns. No Spanish troops challenged their entry. With everything going smoothly, the American commander felt secure in declaring independence for Texas. He set up a government and wrote a constitution.

Earlier, residents living in the Nacogdoches area had built a stone fort. Jane moved into rooms there. In just a matter of days, however, her husband left. The Americans needed military supplies. Commander Long had written to the well-known pirate Jean Lafitte, who lived on Galveston Island. Lafitte was the one person who could supply the guns and ammunition that the expedition needed.

Lafitte had become wealthy by overpowering Spanish and English vessels in the Gulf of Mexico. He had built a large house on Galveston Island. "Maison Rouge" (Red House) was filled with beautiful things he had captured on his raids.

The crafty pirate had not answered Long's request for aid. The American commander felt that he would get the supplies he needed if he talked to Lafitte in person. Long left his wife under the protection of soldiers and made his way to the coast with a dozen men.

As soon as he left, the soldiers at the fort grew unruly. Then news came that 700 Spanish soldiers were approaching. They had been sent to drive out Long's settlement. Panic gripped those at the fort. Jane sent a hasty message to her husband. Then she and the soldiers fled back to the American border.

In Galveston, Long met with Lafitte but got no promises. When word came that Spanish soldiers were advancing on his camp, Long rushed back to be sure his wife was safe. When he got to Nacogdoches, the only person he found was a wounded American soldier. He carried the man back to Louisiana with him.

The Longs reunited in Louisiana, but they received news that the sheriff had seized Jane's possessions. They also learned that Long's younger brother, commander of one of his outposts in Texas, had been killed by Indians. Worse still was the news that baby Rebecca had died. It was a sad journey back to Barbara's house in Alexandria.

CHAPTER 3

Commander's Wife

James Long refused to give up his plans to make Texas part of the United States, but he faced huge problems. He owed large sums of money resulting from his unsuccessful excursion into east Texas. While he was gone, his business had failed, and his partner had made large debts in his name. Friends came to the rescue with money for the Longs to live on, but no one wanted to back another expedition into Texas.

That did not stop James Long. Before many months, he headed to Texas again. This time he went to Bolivar Peninsula, across from Galveston Island.

Jane insisted on going too. In February 1820 she made a short but eventful trip there. Smoking ruins of Maison Rouge greeted her on arrival. Jean Lafitte was leaving. The United States Navy had objected to his activities and banished him from the Gulf of Mexico.

Lafitte's ships were loaded with all his goods. Before he sailed away, though, he invited the Longs to come for dinner aboard his flagship. Long refused to go, but Jane had no intention of missing a chance to meet the pirate. She boarded the *Pride* with another man as her escort.

In her mind she had pictured Lafitte as a rough, unmannered person who swaggered around giving orders. To her great surprise she found elegant furnishings and excellent food. He was not overly tall, but piercing black eyes dominated his unsmiling face. His voice was soft, and his manners were those of a gentleman. They spent a pleasant evening talking. Try as she might to get him to speak about his plans, the pirate told her nothing that would be helpful to her husband.

In order to complete arrangements for the

settlement at Bolivar, James Long took his wife with him to New Orleans. He finally managed to find backers to give him guns and supplies. He was the real leader, but backers insisted that José Felix Trespalacios (trays-pah-LAH-see-ohs) be named as commander. Trespalacios had recently been freed from a Cuban prison. Having him as commander would make Long's entrance into Texas more acceptable to the Spanish authorities.

With money, supplies, and a new uniform, Long sailed to Bolivar. Jane did not linger. She packed dresses fitting the wife of the fort's commander. She took four-year-old Ann to her sister Anne Chesley's house in Mississippi and left her there.

With her husband's friend Ben Milam as escort, she boarded a ship to sail for Bolivar. As they were ready to sail, the customs officer came aboard demanding to search her trunk. Jane indignantly refused and he left.

The ship had barely moved out into the river when Jane changed her mind. She wanted her child with her. Milam hailed a passing boat going upriver, and she boarded it. Once on shore, she hurried to her sister's house to get her daughter. From then on, she kept Ann and her young slave Kian close to her.

James Long and Ben Milam reached Bolivar in June 1820. They began immediately to build fortifications. In a few months, a mud fort took shape. Soldiers mounted a cannon on the walls. It was soon put to use in a battle with Karankawa Indians who lived across the bay.

Long kept good military discipline, and Bolivar was an orderly place. The men built shelters, using lumber provided by Lafitte. The only problem came when Trespalacios put the soldiers to work clearing land. They were insulted. They had come to fight, not farm.

Jane arrived in December with Ann, Kian, and many personal items. Even without a pirate to provide excitement, Bolivar became a community.

Jane planted flowers around her house. She had the companionship of the wives of the two doctors in the group.

News reached Bolivar in the spring of 1821 that the Mexican people had declared independence from Spain. Milam and Trespalacios left immediately to go to Vera Cruz, Mexico, to talk with the leader of the revolution.

San Antonio and La Bahía (Goliad), the only two real towns in Texas, were said to favor independence as well. This provided a perfect opportunity for the Americans to act. With the Spanish government busy putting down the revolt in Mexico, American forces would have no trouble taking Texas for themselves.

Long planned to attack San Antonio and capture the Spanish governor who lived there. Mid-September he marched away with a force of seventy-five soldiers. Fifty other soldiers stayed behind to guard the fort. As he was leaving, Long told his wife that he would be back in three weeks. Jane, who was expecting their third child, promised to wait for her husband at Bolivar.

Before long, a letter from her husband brought cheer to those at the fort. The Americans had reached La Bahía on their way to San Antonio. The town had offered little resistance. Long expected that San Antonio would be just as easy a target. Jane Long did not doubt that her husband would return before their baby was born.

CHAPTER 4

....

Desperate Days

Weeks turned into a month. No word from James Long concerning the expedition reached Bolivar. With no supply ships arriving, food became scarce. Soldiers who had been left to guard the fort grew hungry and discouraged. They began to drift away.

As they left, they took with them equipment and supplies. Jane's friends left too. Finally, a last group of soldiers prepared to leave. They urged Jane to go with them, but she refused. They marched away, taking with them the remaining barrel of flour.

Twenty-three-year-old Jane, five-year-old Ann,

and thirteen-year-old Kian were alone with only a dog for guardian. Still, she did not consider leaving. She had promised her husband she would wait for his return. And that was what she was going to do.

They shot birds, caught fish, and dug oysters to have something to eat. Days grew shorter, and the weather grew colder. Winter set in. The little group shivered as they tried to find food. The dog was as cold and hungry as they were.

On the other side of the bay, fires of the Karankawa Indian camp glowed at night. One day, Jane saw several canoes push off from shore and head toward Bolivar. Desperate to keep the Karankawa from knowing that all the soldiers had left, she and Kian hoisted her red flannel frock as a make-shift flag. They primed the cannon and fired it. The frightened Karankawa turned back.

Christmas drew near. It was bitter cold. Water in the bay froze a quarter mile out from shore. They watched a bear walking on the ice.

Then, on December 21, 1821, on a night when howling wind blew away part of their roof, little Mary James was born. Kian was too ill to help, and

Ann was too young. The next morning Jane was up finding food for them.

The new year was a bleak time, but in early spring a passing ship brought a letter from James Long. He had been captured in San Antonio and was on his way to Mexico City. He assured his wife that he would be treated well since he was fighting on the side of the leaders of the Mexican revolution. He expected to return soon.

More lonely days went by. Finally, there was no more gun powder. No longer able to get birds, they had only fish to eat. Any extra fish they caught went into a barrel of brine to preserve them. When Jane hooked a large redfish, it seemed like fortune had smiled on them. But the fish was so strong that it swam away with the line. Now there would be nothing to eat.

A few days later Kian came running to tell Jane that ships were in the bay. She had seen three men down on the shore. Jane raced after them, but she could not catch them. The men had fled in a panic. They had seen birds sitting on an old wrecked ship and thought that these were Indians.

Dejected, Jane started back to the fort. As she walked along, she spied her fishing line half-buried in the sand. The dead fish still had the hook in its mouth. To her it was a miracle. They would have fish again to eat.

CHAPTER 5

Widowed

The spring of 1822 brought five more ships into the bay. One was on its way to Stephen Austin's new colony about thirty miles inland. Unlike James Long, Austin had permission to bring in American settlers.

The Bolivar settlement, however, was no secret. After Jane attracted their attention, several men came ashore. They were stunned. A heavy-set man blurted out, "You are Mrs. Long?"

The men could see the little family's desperate situation. They asked about food. Jane replied, "I have nothing but that red fish you see drying in the sun."

The men sent to the ship to get bread. It was the first the family had eaten since the soldiers left. One of the men went off to hunt meat. In half an hour he returned with a deer. Satisfied that the family had food, the men steered their ship away.

Other ships brought news about James Long, but the reports were confusing. One said he was one place in Mexico, another a different place. Jane did not know what to think. Finally, a ship captain on the way to Mexico promised to find out the truth. He would let Jane know where her husband was.

Jane had kept her lonely vigil at Bolivar for four months. One day a man she had met in Louisiana rowed by with his family. They were going up the San Jacinto River to make a new home in Texas. They invited Jane to go with them.

At first she refused, and they left an older daughter with her to help. Before many days, their son brought the boat back. Jane placed her trunk on board, and everyone climbed in. The dog trotted along the shore. Jane's extraordinary ordeal was over.

Life among settlers proved to be almost as difficult. The dog drank bad water and died. They lived in a make-shift hut. Ann fished in the little stream to get food.

Then Randal Jones appeared with his brother. The two men built a cabin for Jane. They hunted and supplied meat. In return, Jane and Kian cooked, sewed and washed for the Jones men.

Randal Jones bought a horse, but he had only a $100 bill to pay for it. No one had enough money to make change for the bill. Jane gave him some lace, calico cloth, and a shawl from her trunk to pay for the horse.

In July 1822 the sea captain's letter arrived. With great sorrow, he report that James Long had died in Mexico City. Long had been freed and treated well. He had gone to see a government official. When he put his hand into his pocket to pull out his passport, a guard shot him. The guard said he thought the American was reaching for a gun. Mexican citizens deeply regretted Long's death. Forty carriages filled with mourners followed his casket to the cemetery.

Jane was staggered by this news. Not only was she a widow, but her husband owed large debts. She had no money and no way to provide for her family.

CHAPTER 6

·····························

Hope and Disappointment

Ben Milam and Long's partner Trespalacios had also been captured in Mexico. But the leader of the revolution freed them. Then he made Trespalacios governor of Texas.

Governor Trespalacios sent Jane a letter inviting her to come to San Antonio. The Mexican authorities wanted to provide funds for her family.

Jane was eager to go. She desperately needed the money to pay her husband's debts. She borrowed a horse from the inn keeper, leaving six silver spoons in case she did not return the animal.

Randal Jones and his brother offered to go with her. Their dirty buckskin outfits annoyed Jane. She opened her trunk and gave them some of her husband's clothes. On September 19, 1822, exactly one year after her husband left Bolivar, Jane started for San Antonio.

Riding the innkeeper's horse, she carried nine-month-old Mary James. Ann rode a pack mule, and the Jones brothers shared their horse. Kian and three male slaves walked. Game was plentiful. They stopped for nine days to get enough meat to feed them on the trip.

When they reached La Bahía, residents welcomed the wife of James Long. They held a ball in her honor. Since she was a widow in mourning, she refused to dance. The priest, however, insisted. She relented and danced with him.

After three days in La Bahía, they were ready to leave, but no one could cash Randal Jones's $100 bill. Jane sold an expensive gold watch her husband had given her. She paid the tavern bill, and they set out for San Antonio.

When they arrived, Jane went to stay with Don

José Erasmo Seguín, a wealthy and respected Tejano leader. She stayed there for six months before moving to a place of her own.

The Baron de Bastrop accompanied the Jones brothers when they went to announce Jane's arrival to the governor. Bastrop, a Dutch citizen with a clouded past, was a respected member of the Spanish community in San Antonio.

People in San Antonio were eager to help Jane's family. Friends prepared an elaborate christening for Mary James. They showered the baby with gifts. As part of the celebration, they paid Kian four dollars to walk down the aisle of the church carrying the baby in a long white dress.

It was customary at festivals to give money to the poor. On the way to the christening, friends tossed $100 worth of silver coins to the crowds. But no money ever came to Jane Long from the Mexican government.

Without warning, another revolution broke out in Mexico. The man who had appointed Trespalacios governor was no longer in charge of the government.

Trespalacios hastily returned to Mexico. Before

he left, he gave Jane the guns and swords that had been taken from James Long and his men when they were captured. These were the only things of value she ever received from the Mexican government.

CHAPTER 7

....

Return to the United States

More revolutions rocked Mexico. No government stayed in power long. Troubled times extended all the way to San Antonio. Food grew scarce and expensive. Jane had no money. She felt she must return to her sister Barbara in Louisiana, but she had no way to get there.

Leonard Peck, a well-to-do Philadelphia merchant, came to her rescue. He had known both her husband and Trespalacios. Peck had stopped in San Antonio on his way to Monterrey, Mexico. His train of pack animals was loaded with goods to trade. The merchant promised to take Jane and her family to the United States on his return trip.

Before he left, Peck provided money for Trespalacios to get to Mexico. Knowing Jane's situation, he gave her $500, saying it was just for safekeeping. He made sure she had food before he left. He found two bags of coffee and bushel of corn. He bought all the bread in town one night. When all these things arrived, Jane hid them in her trunk.

Even without money, she refused to take gifts. As Peck left, she insisted that he take some of her rings and earrings. She also gave him two dresses to sell in Mexico. They were equal in value to the things he had given her. The merchant did not try to argue with her. He took the jewelry and dresses, but when he got to the edge of town, he sent them back.

Peck returned a few months later with thirty or forty mules heavily loaded with silver. True to his word, he gathered up Jane's family, and they began the journey toward Louisiana. Jane sold her husband's guns, and on August 6, 1823, she rode out of the city on a fine mare she had bought. The merchant carried Mary James, while Ann rode a gentle mule.

They stopped along the way at various houses. At one place, the man's wife had died two weeks earlier. He feasted them with watermelons and then proposed to Jane. She turned him down.

Near Nacogdoches they were met by Alexander Calvit, Jane's brother-in-law. Three years after Jane had left Louisiana to go to Bolivar, she returned to the Calvit home in Alexandria.

After a stay of six months, Jane decided to visit her sister Anne in Mississippi. Just as she was leaving, Ben Milam rode up. He told Jane how he and her husband had been freed after one of the revolutions. Needing permission to leave the country, they had gone to see an official. The guard shot his friend. Milam fervently believed that Trespalacios had ordered someone to kill James Long.

He had come immediately to find Jane after he returned. On his long journey he had faithfully kept all of James Long's papers and letters. He gave these personal things to Jane, even the suit of clothes in which Long died.

Milam had promised his dying friend that he would take care of Jane and the children. He had come to do that. He mounted his horse and escorted Jane to her sister's house. He stayed in Mississippi for a week.

While Jane was there, tragedy struck again. In June 1824, little Mary James died. A sorrowful Jane returned to Louisiana with Ann and Kian.

CHAPTER 8

....

Land Owner

Texas still beckoned to Jane. Some time after she returned to Barbara's house, she persuaded the Calvits to move to Stephen Austin's colony in Texas. The Mexican government offered 4400 acres of free land to Americans who promised to be good citizens.

In December 1825 Jane, Ann, and Kian, along with the Calvits, arrived at Austin's headquarters. During the three years they lived at San Felipe de Austin, Jane was quite popular. Not yet thirty years old, the attractive widow drew many admirers. A witty conversationalist, she could speak on many subjects. However, marriage was never one of them.

Austin visited the Calvit home. Jane and her

sister made the bachelor empresario a buckskin suit. In response to Jane's special situation, Austin asked the Mexican government to give her a pension. He explained that her husband had helped in the Mexican Revolution. The government refused to grant the request because James Long had not been part of the Mexican army.

Both Jane and the Calvits received land as members of Austin's original three hundred settlers. He assigned Jane property near an old fort at the bend of the Brazos River about thirty miles south of San Felipe de Austin.

Jane's claim to the land was recorded in April 1827. She followed a special ritual to mark her owner-ship. Land surveyors took her by the hand and walked with her around the property. She pulled up a clump of grass and threw rocks to show that she was going to use the land. She planted stakes to show that she intended to build a house and live there. The survey-ors shouted out that she was owner of the land.

Soon, Milam arrived to build her a cabin, but she did not move there immediately. She had no one to help her do the hard work of clearing the land.

CHAPTER 9

Brazoria Boarding House

Within a few years Ann became a lovely young lady of fifteen. Jane wanted to give her daughter a proper education and took Ann back to Natchez to go to school. It wasn't long, however, before Ann fell in love with Edward Winston, and the two soon married.

Jane returned to Texas after the wedding. On the way to San Felipe, she stayed at a tavern in Brazoria. She was appalled at how unsuitable the place was for women or families. She saw a business opportunity.

Brazoria was the port for Austin's colony. Boats

went up the Brazos River all the way to San Felipe. People needed a decent place to stay.

In 1832 Leonard Peck appeared again. He provided money for Jane to buy the Brazoria tavern. She placed an advertisement in the newspaper stating that her new establishment offered rooms for rent, along with meals. With Kian's help, she even did washing. Her place was a respectable one where men enjoyed eating and women could be comfortable.

It was not long before the boarding house with the charming hostess became the favorite place for everyone to stop and eat. Mexican Colonel Juan N. Almonte stayed there while making a tour of Texas. Sam Houston roomed there. William Barret Travis, a brash lawyer who later became famous at the Alamo, often stayed there. When his little boy came to Texas, Travis instructed the escort to take the child to Jane's place in Brazoria.

Everything seemed to be going well until the day a man appeared claiming that Kian belonged to him. James Long had promised to give him Jane's servant if he did not repay money he had borrowed. Jane did not have the amount the man demanded. Before

long, merchant Peck was back to solve the problem, and Kian returned to Jane's house.

Relations between the Mexican government and the American settlers grew worse. Texas settlers asked for more freedom and sent Stephen Austin to Mexico City with the request. Once he got there, he was arrested and put in prison. It was two years before he got back to Texas. When Austin finally returned, Texans celebrated.

A huge crowd gathered at Jane's boarding house in Brazoria. The tables were set three times before everyone was fed. Austin made a speech saying Texans must decide their own freedom. Cheers broke out. Then everyone danced until sun up.

CHAPTER 10

....

Freedom for Texas

About this time Georgia native Mirabeau Buonaparte Lamar stopped at Jane's boarding house. His wife had died, and the lonely widower had come to Texas with $6000 to invest for his friends.

Lamar was not very tall, and people commented on the baggy, old-fashioned clothes he wore. Those who did not know him would never have guessed that he was witty, that he wrote poetry and created oil paintings, and certainly not that he was an excellent horseman and swordsman.

Jane and thirty-seven-year-old Lamar were almost the same age. She was impressed with her guest's keen mind and gift with words. She asked Lamar to give a speech to some soldiers at her boarding house. They were on their way to San Antonio to help fight for Texas freedom.

Lamar was just as impressed with Jane. War with Mexico was looming. He wrote to his brother that if he should be killed in battle, he had left his trunk and valuable papers with Jane Long.

Events quickly turned bad for the Texans. In December 1835 Ben Milam was killed in the San Antonio battle that drove Mexican soldiers out of the town. This insult to the Mexican army made dictator Antonio López de Santa Anna furious. He personally led the army back to crush the rebellion.

Soon, William Travis and a band of fewer than 200 fighters holed up inside the Alamo in San Antonio facing an army of three thousand Mexican soldiers. After bombarding the Alamo for thirteen days, Mexican troops stormed the walls. All the defenders were killed.

Then General Santa Anna moved his army eastward. Settlers fled in panic toward the American border. Jane took her family to Bolivar.

Six weeks after the Alamo disaster, Texans under General Sam Houston faced General Santa Anna's soldiers at San Jacinto. On the day before the big battle, two Texans became surrounded by Mexican soldiers. Mirabeau Lamar made such a daring horseback rescue of the men that even the Mexican soldiers cheered. Houston promoted him to colonel that day, and he was chosen to lead the cavalry.

The following day, in an eighteen-minute battle, Texans shouting "Remember the Alamo" defeated the Mexican army. James Long's dream had come true. Texas was now a free county.

Sam Houston was elected president, with Lamar as vice-president. The new capital was in Columbia, and many important people ate at Jane's boarding house in Brazoria a few miles away.

Lamar spent so much time there that President Houston ordered him to come back to work.

CHAPTER 11

·····································

Meetings with Lamar

In 1837, ten years after receiving her grant, Jane finally began work on her property at Fort Bend. The thirty-nine-year-old hostess sold the Brazoria tavern and moved to Richmond.

She had sold some of her grant to a man who laid out the town of Richmond. Before long, she and Kian were running a popular boarding house there. As Sam Houston's term as president was ending, Lamar's supporters used Jane's Richmond boarding house as headquarters to elect Lamar second president of the Republic of Texas.

Lamar was a man of great integrity, but the new president had grand, expensive ideas. One brilliant idea provided funds for free education at public schools and universities. But efforts to claim half of New Mexico as Texas territory were disastrous.

Lamar's schemes that did not work brought hard times to Texas. Jane, however, survived well. She moved to her land, bought slaves, and began to grow cotton and raise cattle. She registered her cattle brand in Fort Bend Country in 1838. In a few years she had paid off her husband's debts.

After working for twenty years, she owned not only a plantation, but three house lots in Richmond, twelve slaves, and two horses. Seventy-five head of cattle carried her J-L brand.

By the time Jane was fifty, she was one of the wealthiest persons in the state. She had long since gotten back her silver spoons from the innkeeper.

Mirabeau Lamar spent many hours talking to Jane. He planned to write a history of Texas. He especially wanted to tell the story of James Long. Jane told him about her husband and their life together, but the book was never published.

Lamar bought a corner of Jane's property, and the two neighbors planted trees to mark the boundary. They raised cotton as partners. She watched her money carefully. Later their partnership broke up when Lamar complained that she took more than her share of the profits from their crops.

Earlier, a very romantic Lamar had written a poem called "Serenade." The poem compared someone named Jane to the sun and moon. Rumors were that he planned to marry her.

Even at fifty, she remained attractive. She sat for her portrait about this time. Not even the ringlet curls framing her face took away from the force of her personality.

Jane did not marry Lamar or anyone else. A few years later, he rewrote "Serenade" using another woman's name. Finally, he married a young woman from Galveston.

CHAPTER 12

....

Independent to the End

Jane outlived Lamar by many years. She also outlived her daughter Ann. This left her responsible for her
grandchildren, Mary Ann and James Edward Winston.

She was in her sixties when the Civil War came.
Staunchly Southern, she made her clothing from cotton
grown on her plantation. She was especially proud to
knit socks and sew clothes for grandson James while
he fought in the Confederate army.

After the war, the aging grandmother walked
the streets of Richmond, gray ringlet curls sticking
out of her white cap. "Aunt Jane," or "Grandma Long"

as she was sometimes called, usually had a pipe in her mouth.

Time eventually took its toll. When Jane could no longer live alone, she moved to her grandson's house. A second Kian, granddaughter of the one who had been with Jane at Bolivar, took care of her.

Near the end Jane did not leave her room. One day, though, she sat up in bed and told young Kian to get the carriage ready. They took a long drive around Richmond. The first stop was at the house of Jane's doctor. He was startled to see his elderly patient. When he offered to help her from the carriage, she refused, saying he might let her fall.

From there they went to the home of her granddaughter, Mary Ann Miles. Then they paid a surprise visit to Clarissa, Kian's mother. Finally, they drove down the main street in Richmond. Jane stopped the carriage so they could buy ice cream.

About a month later, Kian and her mother lovingly dressed Jane for the last time. The long, exciting journey of the woman who called herself the "Mother of Texas" ended on December 30, 1880.

TIMELINE

1798 ...... July 23, born in Maryland

1811 ...... Moves to Mississippi

1815 ...... May 14, marries James Long

1816 ...... November 26, daughter Ann born

1817 ...... Living at Walnut Hill plantation in Mississippi

1819 ...... Daughter Rebecca born but soon dies;
Long's army driven out of Nacogdoches

1820 ...... Meets Jean Lafitte; moves to Bolivar with
James Long

1821 ...... Long leaves Bolivar in September;
Mary James born in December

1822 ...... April 8, James Long is killed in Mexico City

1822 ...... Honored at ball in La Bahía;
christening for Mary James in San Antonio

1824 ...... Mary James dies

1827 ...... Recording of Fort Bend land granted as
Austin colonist

1832 ...... Opens boarding house in Brazoria; important
persons are guests

1835 ...... Meets Mirabeau B. Lamar;
Stephen Austin give independence speech

1836 ...... April 18, Battle of San Jacinto

1837 ...... Moves to her land in Fort Bend

1838 ...... Registers her J-L cattle brand in
Fort Bend County

1850 ...... 1850–1860, one of the wealthiest persons
in Texas

1870 ...... Ann Long Winston Sullivan dies

1877 ...... Living with grandson James Winston

1880 ...... December 30, Dies in Richmond, Texas;
buried in Morton Cemetery

AUTHOR'S NOTE

Jane Long is buried in Richmond's Morton Cemetery on land that was part of her grant as one of Stephen Austin's original Old Three Hundred settlers. Buried next to her is Mirabeau B. Lamar, with his wife on the other side.

In 1936, as part of its centennial celebration, the state of Texas put a monument on Jane Long's grave to honor the determined woman who played a part in the early days of Texas independence.

The Fort Bend Museum in Richmond, Texas, owns a house she lived in. The museum has her portrait, her piano, and a quilt she made.

Alexander Calvit is listed among Stephen Austin's first colonists. When Mirabeau Lamar wrote Jane's story, however, he spelled the name Calvert. One reason for the difference could be that at that time people were not consistent in spelling words. One interesting theory is that the difference was caused when someone with an accent pronounced Calvert without the "r," making it sound like Calvit. I have chosen Austin's spelling, not Lamar's.

SOURCES

In writing this book, I used information taken down by Mirabeau Lamar during his conversations with Jane Long. What we know of her life at Bolivar is mainly from the things she told Lamar. Lamar never finished the history book about Texas, but the papers from his time as president of the Republic of Texas and his various notes on many subjects were collected into six printed volumes. Jane's story is in volume two.

Fort Bend County has numerous records concerning Jane Long.

--

"This is the handsomest…" Mirabeau B. Lamar, *The Papers of Mirabeau B. Lamar*, edited by Charles Adam Gulick, Jr. and others (Austin: The Texas State Library, 1920-1927), II, 51.

"If you will not take…" *Lamar Papers*, II, 52.

"You force me to choose…" *Lamar Papers*, II, 53.

"You are Mrs. Long?" *Lamar Papers*, II 135.

INDEX